YESTERDAY'S TOYS AND GA

CW01597481

Written by Jack Marlowe
Illustrated by Helen Marsden

Collins Educational
An Imprint of HarperCollins*Publishers*

ANCIENT EGYPT
3500 BC – 30 BC

Toys in Ancient Egypt

Five thousand years ago children in ancient Egypt played with spinning tops made from smooth, flat stones which were spun on their edges. They also played with dolls which had jointed arms and legs and which were made from a variety of materials including clay, mud and straw.

Although most toys were made from easily available clay or mud, toys were also carved from scarcer and more precious wood. Adult Egyptians made models of animals like lions, hippopotamuses and crocodiles.

A wooden pull-along cat with a hinged jaw. Circa 1300 BC. Copyright British Museum.

These toys sometimes had jaws that moved when a string was tugged. Toy horses on wheels were pulled along by a piece of string.

Ideas for other toys developed from tools and weapons used in daily life. For example, adult Egyptians used throwing sticks to hunt for food. The sticks were flat pieces of wood, like boomerangs, but which didn't return when they were thrown. Hunters were very accurate and could hit birds or small animals. Children used throwing sticks like this as toys, throwing them at targets which might be made from circles scratched in the ground or from small piles of stones.

Games in Ancient Egypt

Many people lived near the River Nile and they played water games. One game involved two teams in different boats, using long poles to knock the other team into the water.

Ball games were also popular. Young Egyptians played with a ball made from a leather bag stuffed with corn. These balls were used in catching games where the players leapt into the air or rode piggyback on another player.

Adults and children also played many board games. One particular game was called 'Senet' which means 'pass'. Throwing sticks were tossed to decide moves in the same the way we throw dice now. The aim of the game was to 'pass' from one side of the board (earth) to the other side (heaven) and the players had to defeat 'devils' on the way. This was a little like defeating an opponent's 'knight' or 'bishop' in a game of chess.

Here is an ancient Egyptian game you can try for yourself. It's called 'The Snake Game.'

The Snake Game

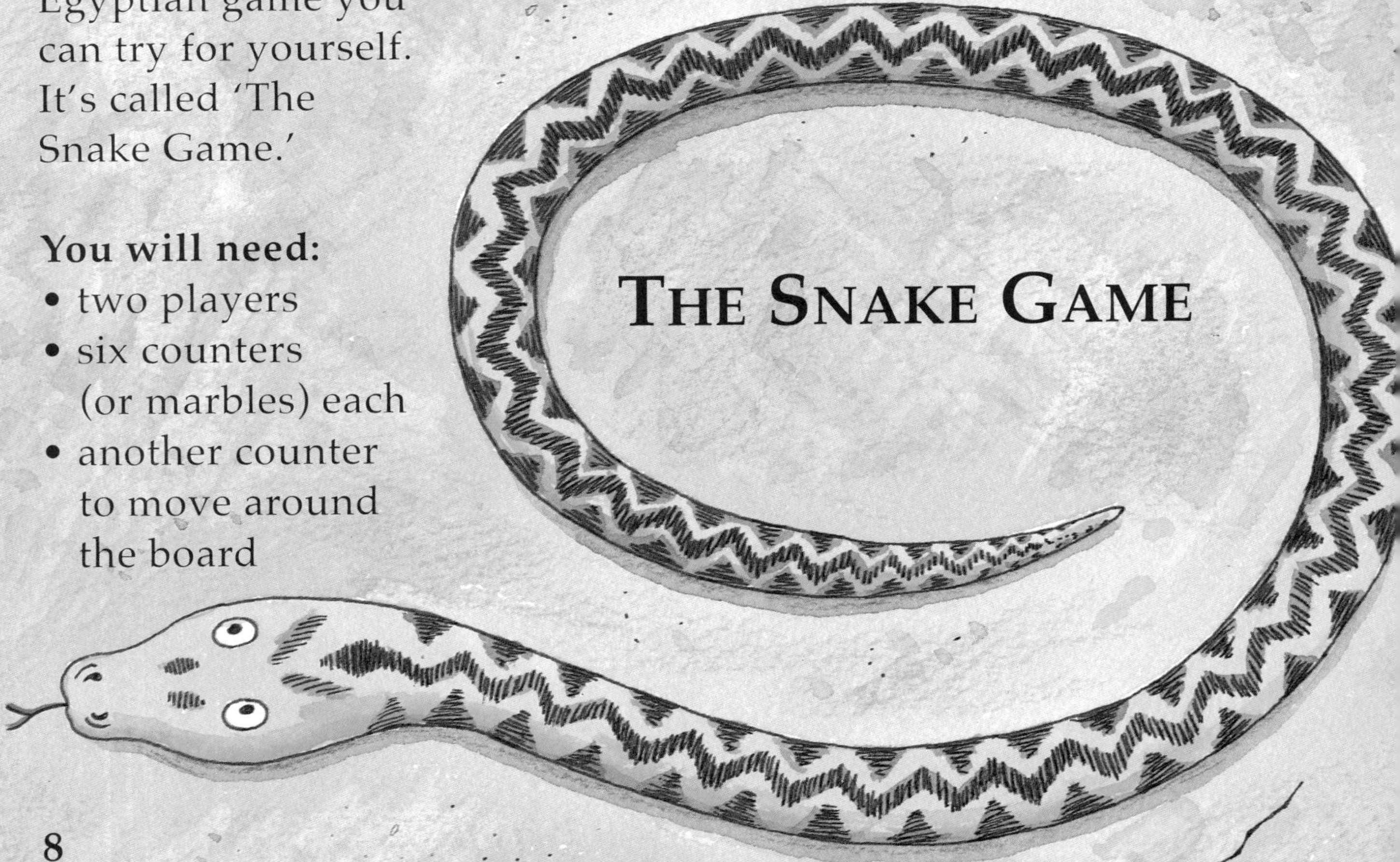

You will need:

- two players
- six counters (or marbles) each
- another counter to move around the board

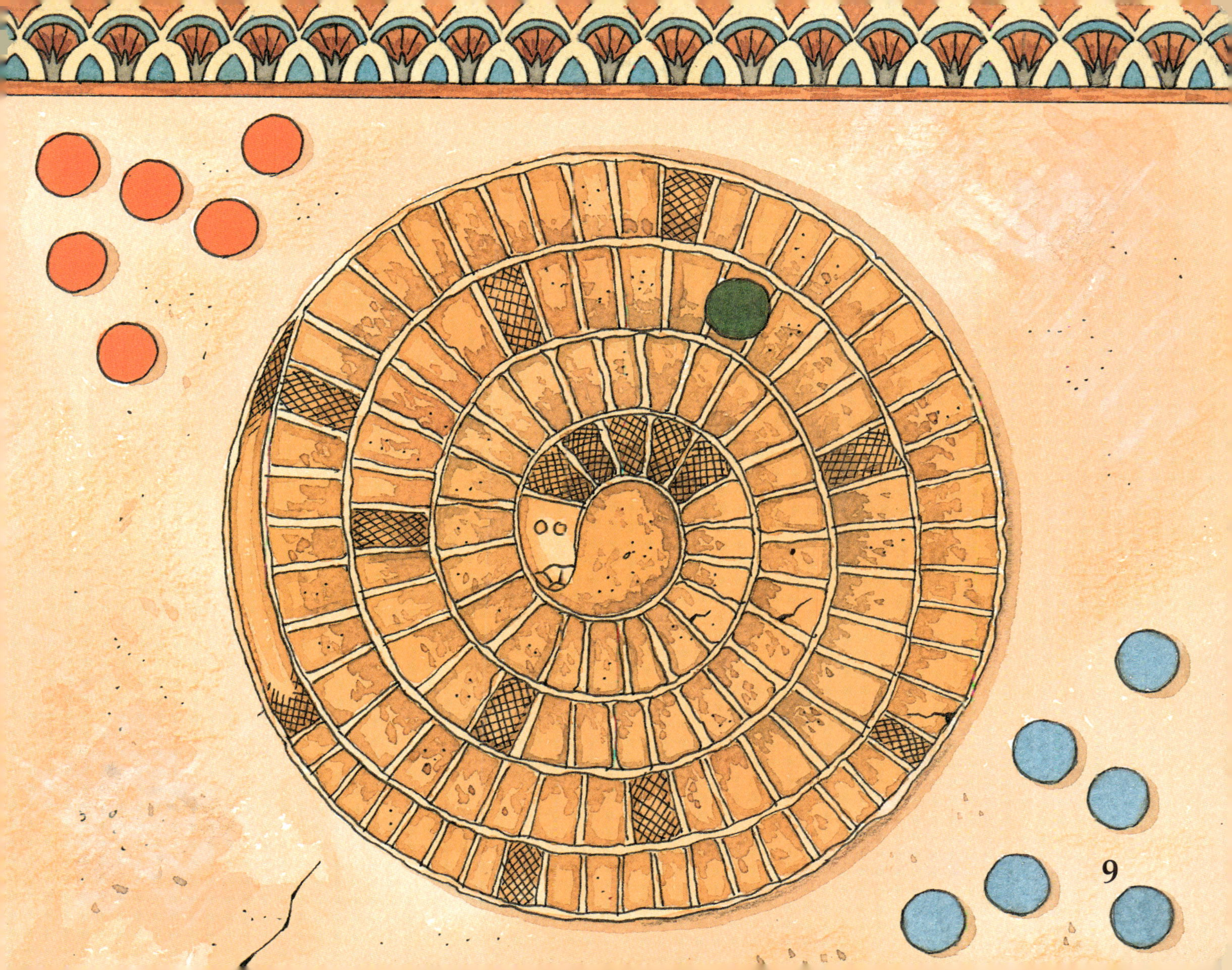

How to play:

1. Decide who goes first and call this person Player A.
2. Player A holds some or all of the six counters. Player B guesses how many counters are in the hand.
3. If Player B guesses **correctly** then Player A scores nothing and doesn't move the playing piece on the board.
4. If Player B guesses **incorrectly** then Player A scores the difference between the guess and the number of counters in the hand. Player A then moves the piece the number of places scored along the Snake.
5. Then Player B has a turn and holds the counters for Player A to guess, score and move, and so on.
6. The first Player to reach the centre is the winner.

For example, Player A has 2 counters in the left hand but Player B guesses 5. Take 2 from 5 and you have 3. Player A then moves the piece 3 spaces.

Ancient Greece
3000 BC – 146 BC

Toys in Ancient Greece

Children who died in ancient Greece were buried with their toys in a burial ritual. The toys might have been their favourites, or they might have been specially made for the child to play with in the next life.

One type of Greek toy that archaeologists have unearthed is a baby's rattle. It is made from clay and is hollow and shaped like an animal. Small clay beads were dropped inside the hollow shape before it dried. Then the toy rattled when the child shook it, just as modern, plastic rattles do today.

A terracotta doll with moveable arms and legs. Circa 350 BC. Copyright British Museum.

Greek children had dolls made from clay which were very similar to those played with by Egyptian children. Greek dolls were brightly painted with moveable arms and legs attached by strips of leather.

Just as today's children play with model cars and aeroplanes, Greek children played with models of chariots. In fact, Greek children played with many of the toys which are similar to those children play with today, including string puppets, toy soldiers, yo-yos, skipping ropes, whistles and hoops.

Greek children stopped playing with their toys when they reached 13 years. This birthday was very important because it showed that they were adults and must give their childish toys up to their gods.

GAMES IN ANCIENT GREECE

The Greeks, like the Egyptians, enjoyed playing games outdoors. Children played at tug of war, on see-saws and they took part in ball games similar to hockey. They also played knucklebones (known today as chuck-stones or five-stones).

The ball games could be very rough. One piggyback game involved two teams fighting for a ball that was thrown between them.

We know about many of these games from paintings on pottery, but don't know exactly what the rules were. In one painting, players throw a ball at a row of sticks. The game looks a little like cricket.

The first Olympic games were held around 776 BC and then every four years after that. At first the games were simply 190m races, or the length of the stadium. At the 14th Olympic Games, another race of twice the length was added. Over the years other new sports were included such as wrestling, where kicking, arm-twisting and jumping on the opponent were allowed; boxing; throwing the discus; long jump, from standing still; throwing the javelin; relay races, carrying a flaming torch for a baton and chariot racing.

There were also Junior Olympics, but only boys could enter these. Girls and women could not take part in the Games and were not allowed to watch.

KNUCKLEBONES

You will need:

- two or more players
- five wooden cubes or dice

(The Greeks used actual knucklebones from the feet of pigs, goats or sheep.)

The aim is to throw five cubes and catch more than anyone else on the back of the hand.

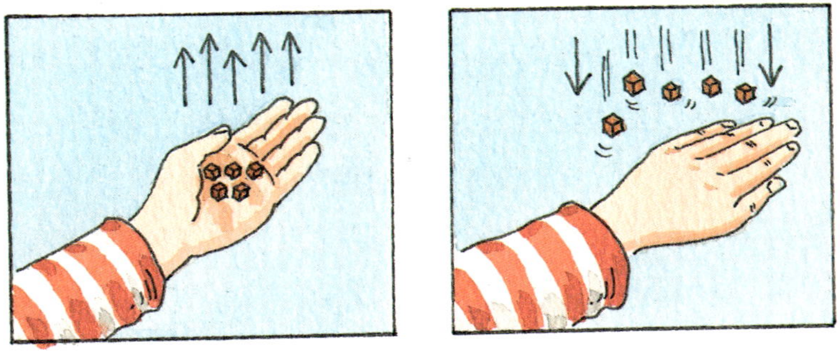

How to play:

1. Hold five cubes in the palm of your hand.
2. Throw them upwards. While they are in the air, turn your hand so the palm is face downwards.
3. Catch as many cubes as you can on the back of the same hand.
4. If they are all dropped, then the next player takes a turn.
   If you drop 1, 2, 3 or 4, then you must pick them up by playing 'ones' as follows.

- Pick up one cube, throw it in the air and catch it on the back of the same hand.
- While it is in the air, pick up another cube from the ground.
- Do this again until all the cubes have been picked up.
- If you drop one then the turn passes to the next player.

The winner is the first to catch all five cubes, either in the first throw or by playing 'ones'.

Ancient Rome

753 BC – 476 AD

Toys in Ancient Rome

In 146 BC the Roman army defeated the Greeks and began to rule in Greece. The Romans allowed the Olympic Games to continue for a few hundred years but the Games were finally banned in 394 AD.

The Romans imitated the Greeks in many ways. The children played with clay dolls and see-saws which were very similar to those used by Greek children. Some new Roman toys included kites, building bricks and swings. Roman children also played with marbles made from glass or clay.

Roman children had toys made from wood as well as model animals and chariots made from lead. (The Romans did not know that lead is poisonous and it is not used in the manufacture of toys today.) Some of their chariots were large enough to carry a child and were pulled along by a donkey.

A painted, wooden pull-along horse.
Circa 200 AD.
Copyright British Museum.

Games in Ancient Rome

Roman children played many of the same games as the Greeks but also invented others which are still popular today, such as Hide and Seek, Tag, Leapfrog, Hopscotch and Blind Man's Buff.

Children invented games from whatever they could find lying around. One game was called 'Nuts'. Each child had some hazelnuts and took turns placing a nut very carefully on a pile. The one who made the pile collapse lost the game. When nuts were not in season, they probably used stones or small sticks for this game.

TRIGON

Here is an ancient Roman game you can try for yourself. It's called 'Trigon'.

You will need:

- two balls
- three players
- a large triangle, with sides about two metres long, drawn on the ground

How to play:

1. One player stands on each point of the triangle.
2. The players decide how long the game is to be played, for example, five minutes.
3. The ball must be passed from one player to another without it touching the ground.
4. The aim of the game is to keep the ball in the air for as long as possible.
5. Players can pat the ball but not actually catch it (a little like volleyball).
6. Then add the second ball so that the two balls are being passed at the same time. (The balls can be passed to either player.)
7. A player who drops a ball loses a point. The winner is the player with the fewest points at the end of the time allowed.

MIDDLE AGES
500 AD – 1500 AD

Toys in the Middle Ages

In 476 AD the Romans finally lost their power to two tribes, the Vandals and the Goths, who attacked Rome from the north and east. A thousand years later the people of Europe discovered America and the Modern Ages began. The period between the Roman Ages and the Modern Ages is called the Middle Ages.

In the Middle Ages many children played with toy soldiers and animals made of clay, as the Romans and Greek children had done. Another favourite toy was a model of a horse's head perched on the top of a stick. This was called a 'hobby horse'.

Clay marbles were made in Holland and children in Britain copied the idea of playing with them. At first children in Britain called them 'bonces'.

In the Middles Ages, great fairs took place where adults bought and sold food and clothes. There were also stalls and entertainers to provide amusements for adults and children. Special toys called 'fairings' were made to be sold at these fairs. A popular fairing was a 'whirligig' which was a brightly-coloured paper windmill that spun around on a stick when the wind blew.

Children also played with the wide metal bands that were wrapped around barrels. They bowled them along the muddy roads of the country villages and the cobbled streets of the towns. When it was windy they also played with kites.

Games in the Middle Ages

From 500 AD to 1100 AD, Britain was repeatedly invaded, first by the Angles and Saxons, then by the Vikings and finally by the Normans. War had a great influence on the games played at this time. Children practised fighting with wooden swords and shields, with bow and arrows and with spears.

Chess was one of the most popular board games during the Middle Ages. Chess was probably first played in India around 500 AD. It was called 'Chaturanga' or 'the army game'. The most important piece was the King and the aim was to capture the enemy king, as in real war.

A King and Queen from the 12th century chess set found on the Isle of Lewis. The pieces are carved from walrus tusk. Copyright British Museum.

Card games were also invented in the later Middle Ages. Many playing cards still show kings, queens and knights dressed in clothes of the late Middle Ages.

In 1348 AD, a dreadful plague called the Black Death killed thousands of people. Children played a game which mimicked the disease. They danced in a circle and sang:

Ring-a-ring a-roses
A pocket full of posies
Atishoo! Atishoo!
All fall down.

The 'Ring-a-roses' was a description of the rash that was one of the first symptoms of the plague, and the 'pocket full of posies' described the flowers and herbs people sniffed to keep away the diseased air to protect them from the plague. The sneeze was an early symptom of the plague before the victims 'all fall down'.

This is a simple game from the Middle Ages. It's called 'Knife-cloth-stone'.

You will need:

- two players

How to play:

1. The players stand with both hands behind their backs.
2. After counting three, each player brings a hand out from behind his/her back. They have made one of these shapes with the hand:

   A pointing finger (a knife).

   A hand spread flat (a cloth).

   A fist (a stone).
3. The winner is the player whose object can destroy the other player's object. So...

   A knife can cut cloth so the knife wins.

   A stone blunts a knife so the stone wins.

   A cloth can wrap a stone so the cloth wins.
4. The player who wins each round scores a point.
5. The first to score 10 is the winner.

TUDOR TIMES
1483 AD – 1603 AD

Toys in Tudor Times

During the period when the Tudor kings and queens ruled England, explorers sailed around the world for the first time and people from Europe discovered America.

Dolls were still popular toys for children, and even the king of France, Louis XIII, played with model soldiers. But there were new and marvellous toys too, including boxes with moving figures to act out little stories. These were called Peep Shows, and were enjoyed by adults and children alike.

A wooden cup and ball game from the mid 16th century. Most modern versions are made from plastic.

Card games, dominoes, draughts and dice were also played by adults as well as children.

Another popular toy consisted of a wooden cup with a ball attached by a length of string, the aim being to toss the ball in the air and catch it in the cup as it dropped.

But one toy which might not have pleased adults so much was a trumpet made from a cow's horn!

Games in Tudor Times

In Tudor times, school lessons went on from sunrise to sunset with only one break for school dinner. There were Christmas holidays and Easter holidays but no summer holidays.

Children from poor families could go to a local teacher at schools called 'Dame Schools'. Wealthy families could afford to send their children to Grammar Schools.

On their rare holidays, children played together in the fields. One game, called 'Stool Ball', was similar to cricket but with a single post for a wicket. The pitch was four metres long, the ball was made of rags and the bat was a stick.

In Tudor times, a version of football was played between two villages. The aim was to capture the ball and take it back to your own village, using any possible means and without following any rules. An eyewitness said:

> *"Every player lies in wait to knock down the other players or punch them on the nose. Sometimes the players' necks are broken, sometimes their backs, sometimes their arms and legs. Sometimes their noses gush with blood. There are no rules that I can tell. The man with the ball must run with it for his life."*

Sometimes football was banned as fights tended to break out among spectators.

One popular game was called 'Merelles'. Try this for yourself.

Merelles

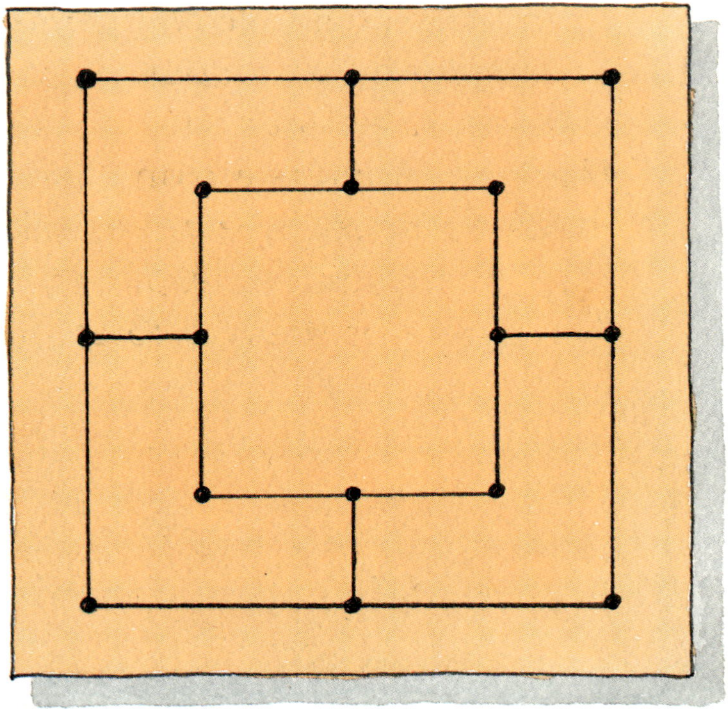

You will need:

- two players
- ten counters - five of one colour and five of another
- board drawn on cardboard

How to play:

1. Each player has five counters of one colour.
2. Each takes a turn to put one counter on a spot. The aim is to put three counters in a row.
3. If all the counters are on the board before one player has made a row of three, then each takes a turn to move one of their own counters. A player can move to any open spot.
4. The winner is the first to get three of their counters in a row.

VICTORIAN TIMES
1837 AD – 1901 AD

Toys in Victorian Times

During Queen Victoria's reign, children from poor families worked long, hard hours in factories for very low wages. They had little time to play and hardly any money for toys. But some factories began to make toys which were sold in shops.

One popular, cheap toy was a 'Gutta Percha' head which was sold in street markets. These heads were made from gum and treacle and shaped into a human head. The head often had a big nose, pointed chin and wide mouth and could be squeezed and twisted by children into comical faces. The heads would eventually return to their original shape.

After an expedition to South America in 1731, scientists became more interested in the material, rubber. It began to be used commercially and children played with bouncing balls for the first time.

Theatre-going was a favourite entertainment of Victorian adults. In imitation, children played with toy theatres, many of which were exact copies of the real ones. Children acted out their own plays using cut-out paper characters and invented their own stories or acted out fairy tales.

Some factory-made toys could be afforded only by wealthy families. Mechanical and clockwork toys such as walking-talking dolls and musical boxes were popular with the rich.

During Victorian times, many railways were built and toy-makers made model railways for tugging along or running by clockwork.

A clockwork bear that would stand up on hind legs and dance. Modelled on bears used by street entertainers at the time. Circa early 20th century.
Copyright Victoria and Albert Museum.

GAMES IN VICTORIAN TIMES

Victorian families were often large. There was no television or radio to keep the children entertained, so 'Parlour Games' were popular on long winter evenings or at parties. One was called 'Whistling Biscuits'. This involved two teams of three or more. Each player had two cracker biscuits. The two teams faced each other and, on a signal, the first player ate their cracker biscuits. When their mouth was empty enough they had to whistle. The whistle was a signal for the second team to eat their biscuits, then whistle. The winning team was the one whose players had all whistled.

CAPTURE

Marbles, made from clay in the Middle Ages, were now made from glass. They remained popular through the 1860s and 1870s and are still sold today. 'Capture' was a simple marble game for two players.

You will need:
Some marbles

How to play:

1. Player A rolls a marble along the ground.
2. Player B rolls a marble and tries to hit Player A's marble.
3. If Player B's marble hits Player A's, then Player B takes that marble.
4. If Player B misses, then the marble stays where it is and Player A tries to capture it using his/her original marble.
5. Player A and Player B go on taking turns until one has captured all the other's marbles.

FURTHER READING

How Children Lived, Chris and Melanie Rice

Dorling Kindersley 1995

How Would You Survive the Middle Ages? Fiona Macdonald

Watts 1995

The "I Was There" Series

River Swift

The Oxford Children's Ancient History, Roy Burrell

Oxford 1994

Teddy Bear Encyclopedia, Pauline Cockrill

Dorling Kindersley 1993

The Tudors (The History of Britain Series), Andrew Langley
Heinemann 1993

Victorian Children (The History of Britain Series), Jane Shuter
Hamlyn Children's 1995

Visual Dictionary to Ancient Civilisations
Dorling Kindersley 1994

What do we know about Greeks? Anne Pearson
Simon and Schuster Young Books 1992

What do we know about Romans? Mike Corbishley
Simon and Schuster Young Books 1991

INDEX

TIME LINE

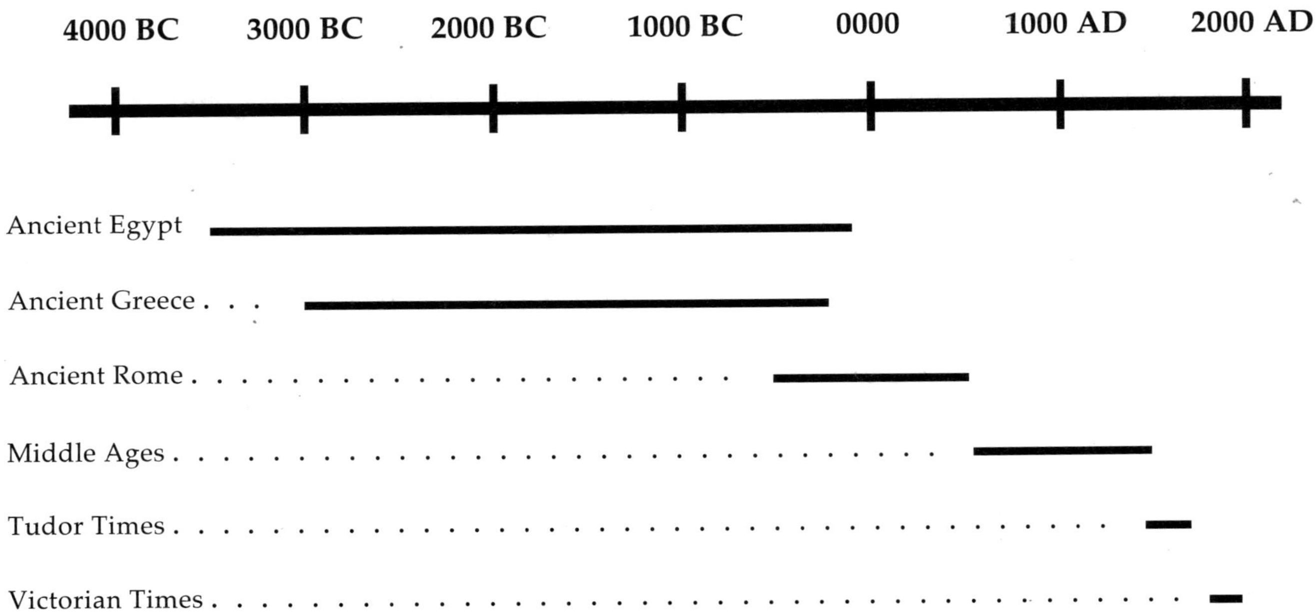
4000 BC
3000 BC
2000 BC
1000 BC
0000
1000 AD
2000 AD
Ancient Egypt
Ancient Greece
Ancient Rome
Middle Ages
Tudor Times
Victorian Times